HEATH ROBINSON'S
GOLF

HEATH ROBINSON'S
GOLF

This edition first published in 2015 by the Bodleian Library
Broad Street
Oxford OX1 3BG
www.bodleianshop.co.uk

ISBN: 978 1 85124 433 1

First published as *Humours of Golf* in 1923 by Methuen & Co. Ltd.
This edition © Bodleian Library, University of Oxford, 2015
Introduction by Bernard Darwin reproduced by permission of United Agents LLP on behalf of Paul Ashton and Philip Trevelyan

Cover design by Dot Little at the Bodleian Library
Designed and typeset in 12/17 Obelisque by Dot Little at the Bodleian Library
Printed and bound in China by C&C Offset Printing Co. Ltd on 157gsm Chinese Huaxia sun matt art

British Library Catalogue in Publishing Data
A CIP record of this publication is available from the British Library

CONTENTS

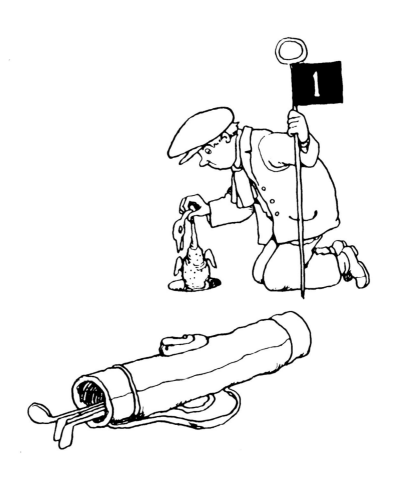

INTRODUCTION

To study Mr Heath Robinson's entertaining pictures is to realize how far more subtle and complex golfing humour has become since the days when the great golf 'boom' first brought the golf joke with it. The mere word 'niblick' was then exquisitely absurd: unadorned it was enough to make any reasonable man split his sides. Of pictorial jests there were two, or at most three. First there was the irascible gentleman represented breaking his clubs; next there were two companion pictures: the first, entitled 'Fore', showed a golfer driving; in the second, 'Aft', a stout pedestrian received the ball on some more yielding portion of his person. Now this is in a sense a primitive and eternal joke. It is like that of an old lady on a frosty day sitting down on a slide on the pavement. If we see it in real life we cannot help giggling, but we soon grow weary of it in a picture. Yet it persisted for years, perhaps because the artist could not trust his public to understand anything more recondite about the game. In this book there is, indeed, one amiable old gentleman who, having broken all his clubs, has tied the head of one of them to his wife's umbrella, but he has not broken his clubs in fury: he has only found the lies on a stony hillside something too much for him. As to the player in front who is hit behind, there is no trace of him at all.

It is, to be sure, hardly right to generalize on golfing jokes from Mr Heath Robinson's pictures, because, whatever his subject, he is never primitive or obvious. His prodigal imagination always soars into more complicated regions. We must look at each of his drawings for some little while before we can take in all his little ingenuities. Only a reader with a most comprehensive eye could get all his chuckling done at once. Sometimes he leaves us half wondering whether we have discovered everything that was in his mind. There is, for example, that picture of the two engaging lions walking away happy and replete, while on the green in the foreground is all that remains of their lunch. There is but one cap, one pipe, one club-bag. Why is that? Does Mr Heath Robinson mean us to infer that the golfer who is so uncompanionable as to play by himself deserves to be eaten? If he ever played on one well-known London course, where every morning a string of old gentlemen follow each other round in single file at the rate of one mile an hour, I can well believe that this was his meaning.

When first we look at the pictures in this book we may think that the golfers whom the artist has created are wholly divorced from reality, but this is not so. Golfers possess imaginations almost as fantastic as his, and some of his flights have in fact been anticipated by real live players.

Take, for instance, the agreeable drawing of a fat man who looks rather like a bandit armed to the teeth. Slung round his waist are various club-heads, and he fits now one and now another to his single shaft according to the exigencies of the game. Years ago there was a golfer who invented one universal club, the heads being affixed, and the degree of loft on their faces varied upon some ingenious screwing principle. The putter on rollers has long since come under the ban of the Rules of Golf Committee. As to the machine called the 'Golf Guider for Hitting the ball on the Exact Spot', I cannot assert that this has ever been made, but one of the most famous of professionals told me that he had often thought of building a kind of spiral groove for guiding the beginner's club-head in the way it should go. Even Mr Heath Robinson's movable bunker exists. At a certain sanatorium in Scotland, where the patients are allowed only a little gentle putting, hurdles on wheels form the hazard, and the course is altered week by week.

I do not for a moment suppose that Mr Heath Robinson had ever heard of these things. His fancy soars on its own wings. He has so provident an imagination as to be quite independent of other people. Therein he is fortunate, because when we come to reckon up the stock golfing jokes of the world, they are fewer than we thought. The jokes about golfers who indulge in paroxysms of rage are now rather antiquated. Golfers have today grown so much better tempered, or at least so much less demonstrative than of old, that they accept their mishaps almost with the impassivity of the professional billiard player. Gone long since is the player who threw all his clubs into the sea, and then, in a fit of remorse, nearly drowned himself in the retrieving of them. Once he had many fellows, but he has them no longer. Gone, too, is that kindliest and most delightful of golfers who once solemnly called down fire and brimstone on a Prestwick putting green, who would administer corporal chastisement to his clubs when they misbehaved, battering his stumpy little putter against the wall with the words, 'You little devil, don't you presume on my good nature any longer!' Where is he who, not content with throwing his bag of clubs into a pond, went back to the club-house, disinterred his reserves from his locker, and made a bonfire of them, feeding the flames, when they showed signs of dying down, with his old boots.

One of the best tempered of my golfing acquaintances once, in cold, deliberate anger, drove several miles to a railway line and watched his clubs being reduced to spillikins by a passing express. Another friend once threw his driver so far and so deep into the whins that he had to say to the couple behind, 'Will you please come on, sir. I've lost my club.'

I always chuckle when I think of him, not without a shamefaced sensation of throwing stones in a glass-house, for I am conscious that my own clubs might sometimes have been lost had there been a gorse-bush handy.

Mr Heath Robinson's golfers do not belong to any particular time or course. True, when I contemplate the drawing of the gentleman about to putt being startled by a small fish leaping out of the hole, I am reminded that in a peculiarly wet winter fish were caught on the fourth green of a London course. But Mr Heath Robinson's golfers are not often likely to be identified with those who play on any course now known to us. They are in their essence impersonal and perennial, and we should be grateful to him accordingly.

Bernard Darwin, 1923

THE FALL OF MAN

A WET SEASON

HOW COAL WAS FIRST DISCOVERED IN SCOTLAND

STYLES IN STANCE—I

SOME FOURSOME

FOR THE WEARY CADDY

AN INTELLIGENT GREEN–KEEPER AT 2.00 A.M., DISGUISED AS AN
EARLY BIRD, SCARING WORMS FROM A GOLFING GREEN

SOME CURIOUS CASES OF LOST BALL

WHEN SPRING HANDICAPS

PYRAMID GOLF

SOME NEW WATER SPORTS FOR THE SEASIDE HOLIDAYS

IMPROVED GOLF CLUBS

MORE IMPROVED GOLF

THE BENT NIBLICK FOR CURLY BUNKER WORK

THE FORLORN HOPE

AN AWKWARD LIE

POGO GOLF FOR 18-HOLE COURSES

HALF TIME

AQUATIC GOLF—I

AQUATIC GOLF—II

THE LOST BALL

AQUATIC GOLF—III

THE TEE

AQUATIC GOLF—IV

HOW NOAH MANAGED TO KEEP HIS HAND IN DURING THE FLOOD

THE SITTING STANCE FOR THE BUDDING PUTTER

SPRING CLEANING OF GOLF COURSE IN READINESS FOR
THE SPRING SEASON

STYLE IN STANCE—II

HOLED!

SHOWING THE UNFORTUNATE EFFECT OF NOT KEEPING YOUR EYE ON THE BALL

ANOTHER AWKWARD LIE

THE RECORD

PATENT PUTTER WITH ADJUSTMENT FOR LEVELLING OUT WORM CASTS

THE ST ANDREW'S BUNKER CHAIR, DESIGNED TO RELIEVE GOLFERS OF THE
NECESSITY OF WALKING ROUND BUNKERS

SOME GOLFING NOVELTIES FOR THE NEXT SEASON—I

SOME GOLFING NOVELTIES FOR THE NEXT SEASON—II

THE NEW ADJUSTABLE TEE

THE NEW GOLF CAR FOR THE COMFORT OF GOLFERS

THE ORIGIN OF PLUS FOURS

RISKS AND LIABILITIES COVERED BY THE NEW 'HEATH ROBINSON' INSURANCE SCHEME FOR GOLFERS

ONE IN TWO
A TRAGEDY OF THE SAHARA GOLF COURSE

STYLES IN STANCE—III

THE LAST HOLE BEFORE THE FLOOD

SOME SUGGESTIONS FOR THE GOLFING NOVICE

SOME INTERESTING METHODS OF PROPAGANDA TO SECURE THE GOLFING VOTE

TO VARY THE MONOTONY OF THE GAME

A NEW ADJUSTMENT FOR GOLF BALLS WHICH SUCCESSFULLY DISCLOSES
THEIR WHEREABOUTS

THE CADDY'S FRIEND

TOO MUCH VIM

APRÉS VOUS

THE ANNUAL GET–THERE–FIRST GOLFING HANDICAP, WHICH SHOULD BE A
FEATURE OF ALL FUTURE GOLF FESTIVALS

THE END